Published in 2016 by:
Spirit Marketing, LLC
700 Broadway Boulevard, Suite 101,
Kansas City, MO 64105

hellospiritmarketing.com
© 2016 Spirit Marketing

Designed in Kansas City by Chris Evans, Steve Duffendack, Chris Simmons, and Patrick Sullivan.

For information about custom editions, special sales, and premium and corporate purchases, please contact Spirit Marketing at info@hellospiritmail.com or 1.888.288.3972.

**Find more ways to color your happiness
at www.handcraftedcoloring.com**

Printed 9/16 in China

Where do you feel at home?

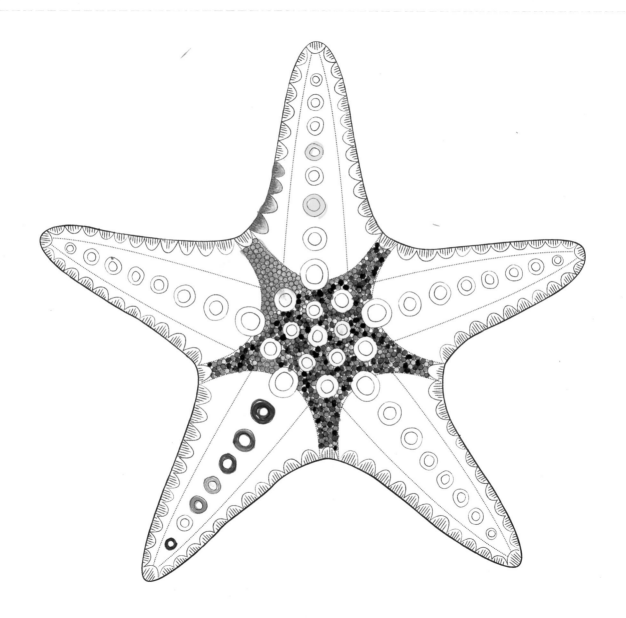

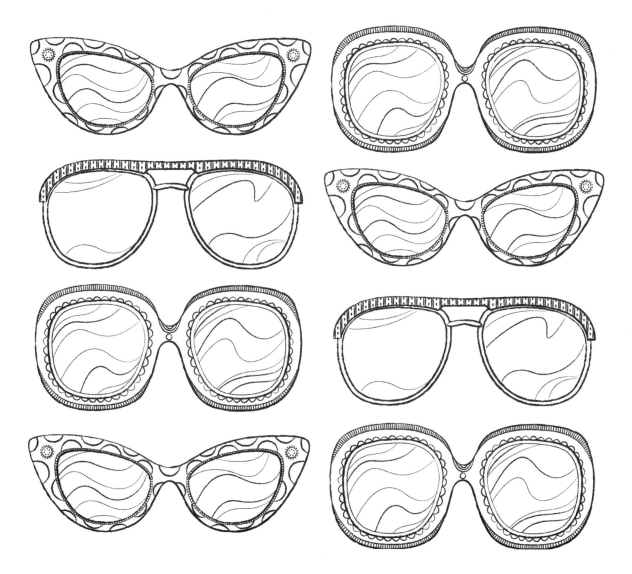

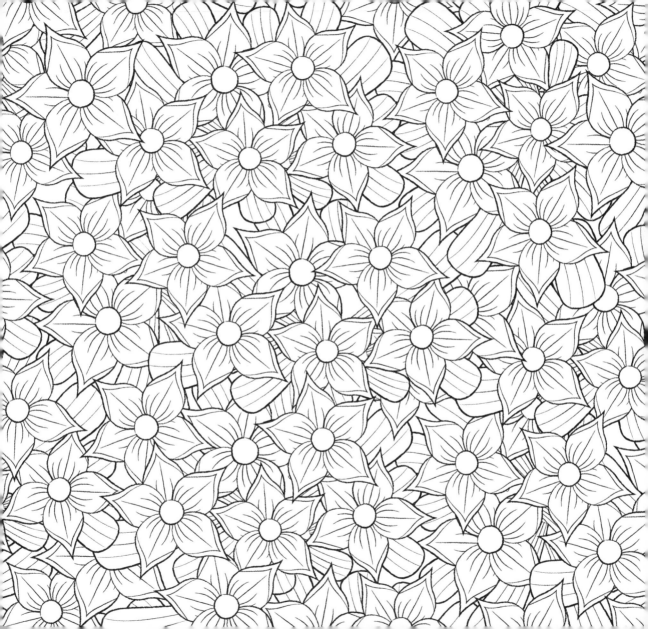

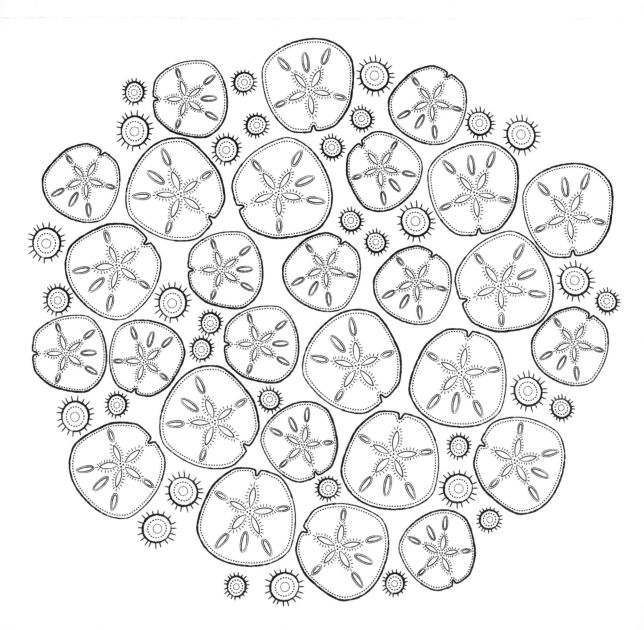

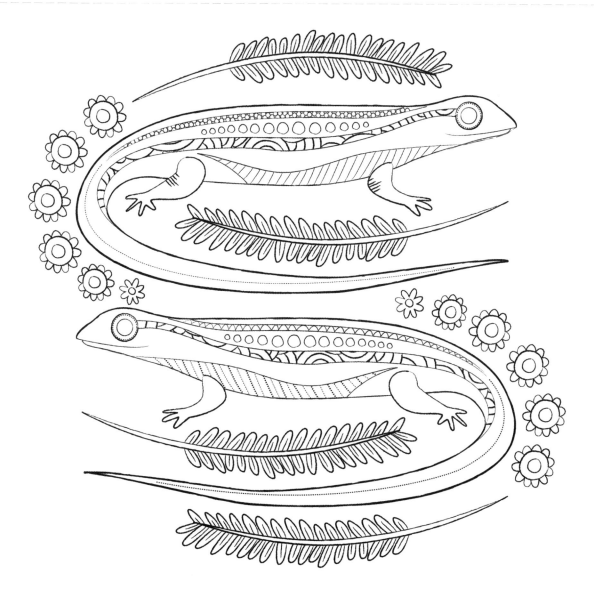

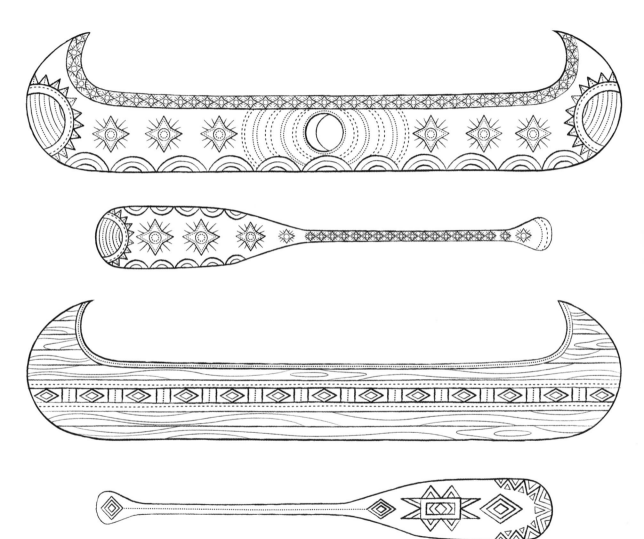